In loving memory

Timothy Luke
"Mr. T"
Nov. 23, 1995-Aug. 1, 2010

"You are forever in my heart"
See you again Soon! Love, Mom

Disclaimer:

Author is not a medical professional, and nothing contained in this publication is to be considered medical advice, but is written solely upon the experience of the author and findings, which occurred through personal experience. Your personal experience may differ from that contained in this book. This book is not intended to take the place of medical care, and all pet owners are encouraged to seek medical attention for their pets to assist them when embarking upon Pet Hospice Care.

This book is intended to help and encourage pet owners who have chosen pet home hospice care as an alternative to euthanasia, and is not intended for any other purpose. It is in no way intended, to encourage pet parents who have chosen euthanasia into changing that decision, should they feel they cannot offer the alternative of pet home hospice care to their pets.

Pet Hospice Care at Home
Loving your Pet through the end

A story of loving, caring, and sharing in the spiritual journey, as your pet approaches the end of life.

Author: Louise Stepherson

Forward

Being a pet mom to multiple pet children over the years, it became clear to me early in my pet parenting, that options and support available to pet parents who are facing end of life decisions for their pets were limited.

Euthanasia is a widely accepted practice for pets, and is often suggested in cases of potentially terminal illness, and more often than not, with no other alternative being offered.

I could never bring myself to make that decision, and quickly learned through experience, that at times, these decisions could be made for you, without your prior knowledge or consent.

I am eternally grateful, that God blessed me with a loving mom, who so graciously opened her heart and her home, along with her great wisdom and assistance, as I embarked upon offering a loving, and peaceful transition for my beloved pet child of almost 15 years, who was facing the end of his life. Without her unconditional love and support, my pet-child could not have received the quality of care we were able to provide him, as we worked together to achieve a common goal, which was to keep him as happy and comfortable as we possibly could, as he made his departure.

It is my prayer, that all pet parents be given the opportunity to offer home hospice care to their pet children nearing their final stages of life; - that euthanasia of pets will no longer be the most common response to terminal illness. It is also my goal that all veterinarian schools offer in depth hospice training as a requirement, and as part of their regular curriculum.

May God richly bless you on your journey, as you offer the loving alternative of home hospice care to your beloved pet child. It is my prayer you will receive the love, guidance, and support you need as you go through the most rewarding experience you could ever imagine;- caring for your pet with unconditional love, at a time when they need you the most.

Chapter One
The Value of a Life

Pets are such wonderful creations. There is always something new to learn from my pet-children. Each one has their unique way of communicating. Each has their individual likes and dislikes. They are individuals, and no two are the same.

It has always amazed me how God created these little creatures so similar to humans. Their appearance is a little different, their ways of communicating is somewhat different from ours, and they use their hands and feet to walk. Aside from these minor differences, their needs are the same as ours.

We all have a need to be loved and accepted. We all have a need for food, water, and shelter. We all have a need to be of value to others. We have a built in desire to please those who love us, and whom we love in return.

Our pets have these same needs. They are no different in this respect. Yet, when facing the end of their life, these needs are too often ignored. So often, the needs of our beloved pets are tossed aside, at a time when they need our unconditional love and acceptance the most.

Society has accepted euthanasia of pets, often prematurely. Many times, it is the only option offered to pet parents when their pets face terminal illness. It is justified, that it is in the pet's best interest. We have believed it to be the loving thing to do. Many pet parents do not agree.

When society so willingly accepts a practice to end life out of convenience, this should be a warning sign for where society is headed as a whole. What will be acceptable next? Where will we draw the line?

I remember years ago before my beloved father passed away from a terminal illness. I made my daily visits to the hospital, doing my best to comfort him, and just be present. It was heartbreaking, as I began to see him little by little fading away, as the end of his life on earth drew nearer to a close. Soon, his job on this earth would be complete. Even still, his life had value. He was still my father. He was still the one who had offered so much to the world. He had retired from the Air Force. He had joined at a very early age, and we had traveled the world as his assignments carried us all across the globe. He had contributed to the freedoms we now have as a society. He had served numerous tours in Vietnam, and Korea. He provided for his family.

After retirement, he became active in the church. He dabbled in real estate investing, and remodeled homes. He taught a multitude of skills to others, sharing his knowledge and wisdom. He spoke with us about God, and the importance of keeping our priorities straight, and not wavering from our faith. Now, he was facing the end of his life on this earth. He had spent months in the hospital in hopes of recovery. He had endured the treatments, and the fact that he was totally reliant upon others for even the most basic needs.

We could not offer a cure, but we could offer our love and compassion. We could not take away his illness, but we could be present to go through it with him. We could not take away his discomfort, but we could gently massage his shoulders and feet. We could not help him out of bed to visit the bathroom, but we could compassionately, give him unconditional love and acceptance, and reassurance that it was okay. We could let him know we were not disappointed. We could let him know we loved him, and accepted him, even in his current state.

Within a few months, as it became more evident that his life was approaching the end, we opted for hospice care.

Lack of understanding always brings resistance

I have to admit, that I have not always been a big fan of hospice. I realize now, that it was my lack of understanding what hospice care was that prevented me from accepting this practice. I embarked upon a journey to learn as much as I could about hospice care, and through this received a spiritual awakening I never would have received otherwise.

I am not very proud of my initial response to hospice practices. I argued with nurses as we settled my father into the hospice house we had chosen. It had been very highly recommended, though I had my doubts in the beginning. I was not ready to accept the methods in which hospice practiced. I had a lack of understanding.

While in the hospital, my father had been on a feeding tube for months in order to receive his nourishment. He was unable to eat, and unable to swallow on his own. The feeding tube inserted into his stomach insured he had a way to receive the nourishment his body otherwise would not have been able to receive. The feeding tube provided a false sense of security. As long as the feeding tube was in place, there was a chance he would survive, and I have to admit, I still had hope that he would one day recover.

Standard practice when leaving the hospital for a Hospice setting is for the hospital staff to remove the feeding tube to prepare the patient for the trip.

Upon arrival to the hospice house, I reminded the staff of his need for a feeding tube. They did not agree.

I became angry, and I was afraid. I began to doubt our decision to place him in hospice care. At the time, I believed they were withholding food from my father. I believed this to be mean and cruel. I did not intend to starve my father, and I was willing to fight to prevent anyone else from doing so. I was determined to get his feeding tube back in place.

There is something so special about those who work in hospice care. They have such great patience, and great understanding of not only the patient, but also the family involved. The nurse on my father's case was very matter of fact, as she explained the condition of my father. She clearly explained what happens when the body begins shutting down, and is no longer in need of food. It was making him uncomfortable. His body could no longer process food. It was literally rotting in his stomach, and causing him a great deal of pain.

In the name of love, I was actually hurting him by my insistence to force feed him, and making his impending death painful, rather than peaceful. I understood now. I agreed that more than anything, I wanted this to be a time of peace and serenity for him. This loving and patient hospice nurse had knowledge I did not have, and thankfully, I listened.

I was present when my father passed away naturally the very same day he had arrived at the hospice home. It was the most peaceful and loving experience, I could ever have imagined. It was a deep spiritual awakening for me, as I witnessed his final breath, and found myself wrapped up in the presence of God Almighty, as his life energy left his body, and he made his transition to a new life, where all pain ceases, and perfect love flows abundantly. It was beautiful. I could not think about my sorrow of him no longer being present in my life. I could not shed tears, other than tears of joy. There was no reason to be sad at that time. He completed his journey, and what a beautiful ending to his journey he had! Shortly before his parting, he raised his hands up toward God, in beautiful worship and adoration.

The presence of God was so powerful when my father passed away. For the next few minutes, in the presence of God Almighty, there was no place for prolonged sadness. There was no place for self-pity. There was no place for guilt. There was only a place for unconditional love,-stillness and gratitude to God Almighty, the Alpha and the Omega, the one and only Creator of all people and all things. God had brought my father into the world, and when it was time, He came to bring him home.

Was there inconvenience prior to this time? I suppose, if you want to call it that. To me, it was an honor;-something I considered a privilege, and something I would not have missed for anything in the world.

Before my father approached hospice care, I took off work and from school more than I probably needed to. I wanted to be available to visit the hospital at different times of the day and evening. I did not want the hospital to know when I would arrive. This was the only way I could assure he was cared for properly at all times. It was my way of keeping the staff on their toes, and it worked by the way.

I soon became the thorn in the side of many hospital caretakers, as I insisted upon prompt care and attention for my father. I soon began offering my assistance with my father when they were short staffed, helping the nurse assigned to my father with bedding changes, and other non-medical needs in which they allowed me to assist. They were grateful for the assistance, and I was grateful that my father was cared for promptly. It also helped free up more of the staffs' time in order to offer better care to the other patients. It was a win-win situation for all concerned.

I learned so much during my journey with my father as he approached the end of his life on earth. I learned the value of life to the very end;-the value of putting yourself aside for just a while, to love and care for another living, breathing creation of God. The lessons I learned were priceless, and ones I would carry with me from that point forward.

My father was a pet-parent, and had many little furry children through the years before he passed away. Little did I know at the time, that what I had learned during his spiritual journey, would allow me to offer the same, loving and respectful care to my pets as they began their spiritual journey toward the end of life on this earth.

Chapter Two
Choosing Pet Hospice

I knew something was seriously wrong with Timothy. He had begun limping a week prior, though it was inconsistent. My first thought, was that he must have something in his paw. I checked him from head to toe, and found nothing. I decided it was probably nothing serious, more than likely something simple that happened during play. Deep down inside, I knew better. Still, I decided to give it a day or two to see if it subsided.

I noticed that at times, he was walking fine. Then, again, I would notice him limp, ever so sporadically. My suspicions were beginning to surface, though I did not want to accept the thoughts that were running through my mind. I began checking for bumps or protrusions on his leg that would give me a clearer indication of what we were dealing with. I kept praying that it was only his age, that at most, it was a bout of arthritis. He had been with me over 14 years. It was a familiar path, and one I was not yet prepared to take.

I was so grateful for each day with him, though I knew deep down inside, I needed to prepare myself. My last chow had passed away at 15. I had almost lost Timothy almost six years prior from an internal abscess. There were no visible signs, and he never showed any indication of illness, until one day, he stopped eating. A few short weeks later, and multiple trips to the veterinarian, it was confirmed he needed surgery. It was his only chance for survival.

I will never forget how afraid I was. The thought of losing him at only 9 years old was more than I could fathom. He was the absolute light of my life, and I would do anything, at any cost, to save my precious baby.

Almost 6 years later, these fears began to surface again. I had cherished every single moment I had with him, and though the thought of losing him was more than I wanted to accept, this felt different somehow. It felt final. I could feel it with every ounce of my being.

As Timothy began limping more consistently, a visit to the vet confirmed my suspicions. Timothy had bone cancer. The origination was in the clavicle area, leaving the possibility of amputation of the limb and chemotherapy as a cure not to be an available option.

I brought Timothy home. I wanted to do more research for available options, and I needed to plan for the time his job on this earth would be complete.

I spent countless hours on the internet, on the phone, and sending emails to anyone and everyone who may be able to offer me the guidance and direction I needed. There was so little information available as to how to care for a pet with bone cancer; I feared my caring for him would be a shot in the dark. Even still, I knew euthanasia was out of the question. He deserved better. He was my very best friend. He was worth everything to me.

As I sat in silence, watching him in his peaceful slumber, the answer came. It was the only answer that gave me any peace. I came to terms with the fact that I could not save his life, but I could insure that he was happy, safe, loved, and nurtured to the very best of my ability.

With extremely limited information, I opted to follow my heart, reaching deep down inside out of the love for my pet, relying on that love and the natural instincts of a loving mom. It was important to me, to offer him the care and support he deserved as he approached the spiritual journey of transition from this life, to a new life where he would be free from pain, and once again, become whole.

Timothy had brought so much joy into my life. He had loved me unconditionally; even during times, it was hard for me to love myself. He taught me the true meaning of an unselfish love. If I could not save him, I at least wanted to offer him the same unconditional love and acceptance he had given me for so many years. I wanted to love him, care for him, and nurture him during this time, even when he could not give back. He still was so happy. He still had so much love to give. He was not ready to let go of me, and I certainly was not ready to let go of him.

As with any parent, I made my mistakes along the way, and it is through those mistakes that I could look ahead, and begin anticipating his needs before it became an actual need. God was with me every step of the way, as I would prepare for the next circumstances, even when I did not realize at the time why or how it would be useful in our journey. I was so very fortunate, to have a loving mom, who so graciously and willingly, opened her heart and her home to us, and played a major role in coming up with solutions to new challenges we faced. She helped provide a loving, caring, and nurturing environment, and supported me in my decision to go through this transition with my beloved pet child to the very end. She helped care for him when I had to leave the house, and got up with us in the middle of the night, when he needed bedding changed. She anticipated his needs, sometimes more successfully than I did, and came up with creative solutions to meet the daily challenges we faced.

Having support is very important to anyone who chooses to offer home hospice care to a pet. It is a very special and precious time in the life of your pet. It is also a very emotional time for your pet and for you as well.

Call upon a family member or close friend whom you can depend on to offer you the encouragement you will need. Ask if they would be willing to come by to visit with you, and help you during this time.

A few organizations are happy to offer their wisdom and support as you embark upon this spiritual journey with your pet. You can do an internet search to find them, or visit our website, which has these organizations listed.

Having someone, you can call who will be dedicated to helping you see this through to the end will be a lifesaver for you. Family or friends who have been close to your pet are your best resources. Your veterinarian may offer names and phone numbers of those who are willing to offer their assistance during this time as well. I was blessed with a very loving and willing mom who loved Timothy as her own grandchild. She was an absolute lifesaver to us during this time.

The end of life takes on many different stages. Some are very subtle, yet recognizable if you are in tune with your pet. By spending as much time with your beloved pet during this transition, you will become connected on an even deeper level, having a greater ability to determine the ongoing needs of your beloved pet.

With each stage, a new challenge will arise, and new solutions will come with them. You do not need any special qualifications to offer your pet home hospice care. The only requirement is a true love for your pet, and the ability to realize that they deserve the same loving care, acceptance, and humane treatment that any other person would receive while approaching end of life.

The end of life is a spiritual journey, and is not to be taken for granted. Timothy deserved the opportunity to travel this journey, - to be lovingly, and gently taken home in God's time. I would not want that taken from me, and I was not taking this from him. It was one of the

most rewarding experiences I have ever had the
privilege to be a part.

What is Pet Hospice Care?

Pet hospice care is not a widely known practice, though it
is making its way around the globe, as more and more pet
parents are searching for alternatives to euthanasia.
Many pet parents, not having the option of hospice care
presented to them, have grieved many years for their
beloved pets, after being convinced that euthanasia was
their only option. Many of these pet parents admitted to
having feelings of profound grief, which lasted several
months to up to a year or more, along with guilt of having
to euthanize their pets. Many were not given the time
they needed to come to terms with losing their beloved
pet. They were not given the opportunity to show their
pet the same love, gratitude, and acceptance their pet had
given them. They were left feeling empty and hopeless,
as they were encouraged to end the life of their pets
prematurely, even when their pets had so much life left
inside of them, and so much love left to give, and love
left to receive in return.

Pet hospice is a labor of love. It is no different from
human hospice care. Pet hospice is giving your beloved
pet the opportunity to travel the spiritual journey toward
the end of their life on earth. It is a way to give your pet
the most precious give you could ever imagine,-the
opportunity to pass away naturally, in Gods' time, and the
opportunity to experience the beauty of the spiritual
journey that occurs during the end of life. Pet hospice
can be the most loving and rewarding experience, you
could ever have in this lifetime. It allows you and your
pet to go through this transition together, giving you and
your pet the opportunity to say good-bye over a period of

time. It allows you to offer the unconditional love and care to your pet during a time they need you the most. It is a precious time of developing and even closer bond of unconditional love and acceptance with your pet that has given you so much, and asked so little in return. They need you to do this for them, the same way they would do this for you, if they could.

Pet hospice is palliative care. It is not expecting a cure, but keeping your pet as comfortable as you possible can in a loving environment during their transition. It is loving them unconditionally, all the way to the end.

There are a variety of ways you will be doing this, such as offering pain medication when needed, tending to their nourishment, assisting them in bathroom breaks, and keeping them clean and groomed during this time. Just as importantly, is spending quality time with your pet.

As your pet begins to progress toward end of life, you will be changing bedding, keeping them turned and repositioned to keep them comfortable and prevent bedsores and giving them sponge baths to keep them clean and odor free. Pet hospice is all about your pet and their comfort. It is about giving them unconditional love and acceptance, placing your own feelings aside, and allowing them the freedom to progress to each stage naturally, without reservation.

Is euthanasia still an option after beginning pet hospice care?

At any time during the course of pet hospice, the pet parent is free to opt for euthanasia should they choose to do so. I would strongly encourage you to search your heart, and be honest about the real reasons you would consider euthanasia over continuing pet hospice. It is not uncommon to feel overwhelmed, especially in the final stages of their life. It is not uncommon to second-guess your decision, especially when their time is nearing the end of life.

I have not seen a single person or pet, who when approaching the end of life was happy, joyful, and playful.

We have a tendency to make decisions sometimes based on our emotions at the time. Yes, we want to see our pets happy and joyful as they once were, but that is not possible when nearing end of life. They are resting, and going through a spiritual and emotional time of letting go. It is important to remember, that this is not about us, it is about loving our pets to the end, at each phase, and giving them the freedom to progress naturally in Gods' time.

I have heard of some pet parents opting for euthanasia for a variety of reasons. Some have listened to the advice of others who do not understand the bond between a pet parent and their pet, and do not understand the concept of pet hospice care. Others have families who were not supportive of pet hospice and all it entailed. Still others were unable to take the time off from work once their pet progressed in their journey toward end of life. Some found providing pet hospice care to their pet was too emotionally painful for them. Others chose euthanasia due to the low cost, and the ability to plan the death of their pet around their schedule, rather than allowing the natural course to take place.

In our current society, all employers do not offer paid sick time or vacation that can be used during this time. As pet hospice becomes more widely accepted, more pet hospice caregivers are on the horizon. If you cannot personally offer pet hospice, you can check with your veterinarian. They may be able to give you contact information of someone in your area who offers this service. Do not stop with your own veterinarian. Call

every veterinarian in the area. More than likely, you
will find at least one of them who can offer you contact
information for someone who is ready and willing to
offer your pet the love and care they need during this time
of transition. Many will come to your home to train and
assist you in hospice care, even sit with your pet during
times you have to be away. Others may offer pet hospice
care in their homes. You would be taking your pet to the
caregiver, for them to love, care for, and nurture your pet
as they approach the end of life. Pet parents are always
welcomed to visit, and are encouraged to do so. With
these options available to offer pet hospice care for your
beloved pet, euthanasia can soon be no longer the
acceptable method of choice. Even if you cannot be
present in the daily needs and care of your pet, you can
still offer them the opportunity to experience a natural
and spiritual parting, the way God intended. You can still
offer them, this final gift of love.
I would encourage anyone who truly wants to give their
pet the care and nurturing they need during end of life, to
resist what others think or believe to influence them in
any way. It is important to remember, that you are the
one making the decision, and you will be the one who has
to live with the choice you made. Others do not have to
understand, and it is not our job to make them
understand. If you truly want to offer pet hospice care to
your beloved pet, I would encourage you to do so. Others
can either accept it, or not, but it does not have to change
your decision. Pet hospice care is a personal choice, just
as the choice of euthanasia. I encourage you to make the
choice your own, and be at peace, with the choice you
make.

Chapter Three
Early end of life stages

There are many stages to the end of life, many of which are so subtle they may be difficult to recognize. The actual beginning stage of end of life occurs before any symptoms have presented themselves. During this time, there is no way you could possibly know anything was wrong. For the sake of not complicating things, we will refer to Stage 1, as the onset of noticeable symptoms.

Stage One

When dealing with terminal illness, or nearing end of life symptoms due to age, this is the beginning of noticeable symptoms that something is wrong. It may be a limp, whimpering, tiring more easily, or discovering a noticeable bump on your pet that proves to be cancerous. Whatever symptom they are experiencing at the time, once this first becomes noticeable, and your veterinarian has confirmed terminal illness, this is considered the beginning. This is also the time when most pet parents take their pet to the veterinarian. Tests are performed, and at times, pre-determinations are made while awaiting test results. Prescriptions may be offered while waiting. Diagnosis is often made during this stage, and treatment options are discussed. It is also during this time, when some pet parents make the decision to either treat the illness, or allow it to take its normal progression. Much of this is determined by the age of the pet, and what the treatment entails.

Many treatments, such as chemotherapy in an aging pet, could potentially do more harm than good, and would not be overall beneficial to the pet or the family. It is important that you ask your veterinarian to set time aside to speak with you in depth regarding various treatment options and what the specific treatment would entail. You will also need to know what this will put your pet through, versus the quality of life your pet would have during treatment, and the overall prognosis.

The end needs to justify the means. Ask questions. Do your homework. The better informed you are regarding your pets' illness, the more likely you and your veterinarian can work together as a team toward solutions to treatment and care. If hospice care is decided upon, you will need pain medication from your veterinarian to keep your pet comfortable, especially as the illness progresses.

Not all Veterinarians are created equal

I have found the above statement to be true in some cases. Not all veterinarians have the knowledge of pet hospice care, and not all of them are supportive of it. Many are not trained in pet hospice, and are not familiar with the concept. It is important that you retain the services of a veterinarian, who supports you in your decision to offer pet hospice care. They do not necessarily need to have formal training in pet hospice, but a willingness to accept it, and learn hands on, and be supportive to you during this time. They also have a wealth of information that will help you in keeping your pet as comfortable as possible.

Recalling an incident with our pet rabbit;- living in the city at the time, we were forced out of convenience, to visit a veterinarian we were not familiar with, due to time restraints and the length of the trip to visit our familiar veterinarian. Our pet rabbit of 12 years was diagnosed with cancer. The veterinarian immediately told us under no uncertain terms, that we would have to euthanize him. Upon our refusal, she insisted we sign a statement of refusal to euthanize. We did not sign it. We did not have to. It was our choice.

Soon she came into the room with a prescription she told us to give the pet rabbit. We should have recognized the warning sign. As hard as it is to fathom someone would rob us of our chance to offer loving care to our pet rabbit of 12 years, I believe she had. We should have done our research. We should have asked more questions. We should have insisted on knowing exactly what the medication was, and what it was being prescribed for. Even in our dislike for this veterinarian, we trusted her to respect our wishes. Instead, I believe she chose to end life prematurely. There was nothing more I could believe. He was still so happy and vibrant. We took him home and short while later, following the medication he passed away.

I am not sure how common of practice it is for a veterinarian to take matters into their own hands. Unfortunately, a veterinarian is within their right to do this, at their discretion.

Do your research. Talk to different veterinarians and find out their position on pet hospice care. It is important if you are to offer pet hospice for your pet, that you get your veterinarian involved in order that pain medication can be prescribed, and you have the support you need in your desire to offer your pet the natural course of life, which includes end of life care.

Check out prescriptions before giving them to your pet if you are not familiar with your veterinarian, or are forced to use a veterinarian while out of town. Check the name against what the prescription is normally prescribed for. Call a pharmacist and ask for information on the drug should there be any doubt in your mind, especially when dealing with a veterinarian in which you are unsure.

Many times, during the first stages of terminal illness, your pet is still eating and drinking normally. They are normally still rather playful and active, showing little sign of illness. They will tire more easily, and although they seem to manage very well, they need help at times going to the bathroom to prevent them from falling. During this time, they are still determined to do things on their own. If limping is an issue, it is time to close all doggy doors and keep them closed. You will need to be sure you schedule your time to take your pet outdoors for potty breaks at regular intervals. This can be nothing more than taking your pet outside in the morning before leaving for work, and arranging to come by during lunch. Of course, you will want to be sure you come home after work, before planning after work activities.

Once your pet is limping, or falling frequently, it could progress rather quickly. It is very possible, your pet could be stuck in the pet door while you are away, having no way out. Their bones are becoming much more brittle at this time, so you would want to prevent situations, which could cause potential harm. This is a good reason to keep doggy doors closed.

During the early stage, you will more than likely only have to make concessions to schedule regular times to take your pet outside for potty breaks, and be sure you keep food and water nearby your pet.

If your floors are not carpeted, this can make it more difficult for your pet to get around. Often they need the traction the carpet provides to help them maintain mobility for a longer period. Consider purchasing a large, inexpensive throw rug for the area where your pet will be. You will be removing this later, but in the earlier stages, it will provide a way to help your pet with mobility to continue to access food and water, so long as it is close by. If you do not have one already, you will need to consider a pet bed, which is low to the ground and comfortable. Your pet will need a soft, comfortable place that is easy to get in and out of, without the risk of falling. You do not have to buy an expensive pet bed. Later in the book, you will find inexpensive ways of creating your own pet bed, should you not have one.

Pets should be kept close to the main activities of the family during this time. They need to feel as though they are part of the daily routines and need to be close to those they love during this time. In the early stage, they do not necessarily need your constant attention, but they do need your presence. Keeping them in the main living area where most activities take place will keep them happier during this time of transition.

Consider the size of your pet

The size of your pet will often determine the length of time your pet has to spend with you before the end of life approaches. Larger pets tend to have a longer transition, while smaller pets seem to make the transition more quickly. This is also dependent upon the type of illness your pet has been diagnosed with, and any other potential health problems. Often, it is not the disease that ends the life of a pet, but the complications of the disease. Cancer can spread rather quickly in pets when opted to let things take their natural course. In many cases, a prognosis of 2-5 months is average, provided diagnosis was made in the early stages.

Normally, the noticeable sign of cancer spreads a little slower in the earlier stages, picking up a more rapid pace during stage 3. This is just a guideline, and your pet may experience individual circumstances depending on his otherwise overall health.

26

Keep an Activity Chart

An activity chart will be a very useful tool for you for many reasons. It will help you be able to have a clear picture of what is going on with your pet, and give you telltale signs of the progression of their illness. It will also help you determine which times they need someone with them the most, when they ate, how much, and when they went to the bathroom. This chart will also come in very useful for your veterinarian who is assisting you in your journey to provide hospice care for your pet. It is a useful tool for other caregivers, so everyone will know what has occurred, and any action taken. It is very important to log any medications given along with the time and dosage. Behaviors are also good to put on the chart, such as "sleeping peacefully" or "licking lips, offered water, went back to sleep". Or "seemed uncomfortable, turned over, resting peacefully", or "bowel and bladder" to indicate bathroom habits. I have included a sample of an activity chart I have used. It worked out very well, and I cannot imagine taking care of a hospice pet without one. It is not necessary you use a formal chart;-an inexpensive note pad will do just fine.

Activity Chart
(Example)

Date	Time	Behavior/action	caregiver
11/1	11:30	ate lunch-appetite normal	LS
11/1	1pm	bladder-bowel-sponge bath	LS
11/1	1:30pm	162 mg baby aspirin-pain	LS
11/1	2:00pm	sleeping peacefully	LS
11/1	6:00 pm	dinner-appetite normal	LS
11/1	7:00	bladder/bowel	LS
11/1	7:45	81 mg baby asp.-preventative	LS
11/1	8:00	sleeping peacefully	LS

Notes: (example) slept a lot today. Was awake for a while, looked comfortable and happy. Looked as though he was in deep thought much of the time. Responded well to my voice. Brushed his hair gently, - seemed to enjoy it thoroughly, fell asleep as I was brushing his hair.

Stage 2

During this stage, you will see changes that are more noticeable in your pet and their behavior. They may tire more easily and sleep more. Although they still have their normal appetite for the most part, at this stage, it begins to come and go. Increased thirst is normal; therefore, it is important you keep plenty of fresh water available at all times. You may notice more difficulty in walking, noticing them stumble often. You may notice them lying on the floor, paws spread out, giving you that embarrassed type of look. They may also begin crawling, as they attempt to get to the water or food bowl, or attempt to get to the door to let you know they need to use the bathroom. They need your help. They need your understanding. They need your love and your unconditional acceptance. They may have an accident on the floor, because they could not get to the door to tell you they needed out.

They need to be reassured that you love them, that you are still proud of them, and that this is okay. During this time, they will need your help to go outside safely to the bathroom. You will need to offer gently support as they are using the bathroom to prevent them from falling. Often times, they still have the desire to do things on their own, however they are unaware that their bones are becoming more fragile, and can easily break should they fall.

You may offer support by cupping your hands together beneath their upper abdominal area, near the rib cage, and very gently offering support, being careful not to actually lift them, which would cause them to be uncomfortable due to the pressure. You can also use a wide piece of cloth beneath their abdomen, holding onto each side, offering a very gentle lift. You do not want to lift too much, as you could topple them forward, causing them to fall. Just offer gentle support, being their safety net, should they lose their footing or balance, or become weak.

It is important, that throughout this transition, you reassure them you understand, that you are not disappointed in them, that you love them and are proud of them.

This is also the time to come up with solutions to help transport larger pets outside to the bathroom when needed. Smaller pets can be gently carried outside, while larger pets prove more of a challenge.

My mom came up with the most wonderful solution to transport my beloved pet during this time. Already having a ramp built onto her home, which was used by my late Dad, she created a pet slide using inexpensive materials. Using an inexpensive portion of a 4x8 sheet of the plastic shower panels sold in home improvement stores, we attached a 1x3 board, the width of the panel, attaching it with screws, using washers to prevent it from pulling through to one end of the panel. We then drilled two holes, and inserted a rope, tying the ends on the back of the board to create a handle. Within 5 minutes, we had an easy, inexpensive, and effective way to transport my pet up and down the ramp for his bathroom breaks. It proved to be the easiest thing in the world to care for him during this time.

Having him on a blanket, we simply slid the blanket with him on it, onto the slide. We then pulled him down the ramp, helped him to use the bathroom, and then gently guided him back onto the slide, laying him on his blanket for the trip. He was so happy to be able to go outside to go potty. He was still very alert and responsive during this time, and it gave him great pleasure to be able to do some of the things that made him feel good about himself. We received a lot of use out of this inexpensive solution, and the joy and happiness it brought into his life was priceless. Sometimes he wanted to linger and sit outside for a while. Knowing he could not protect himself in this condition, I would grab a soda or cup of coffee, and sit with him. Sometimes I would bring a book with me outside, and we would enjoy spending the time together, as he gazed at the sky and the beauty of the outdoors as I read my book. Sometimes, I would sit on the ground with him, and would sing his favorite songs, and other times, we would gaze at the clouds in the sky together and just talk. Absolutely some of the best of times, and ones I will forever cherish in my heart.

Guarding the dignity of our pets

One of the most common misconceptions I hear regarding pet hospice care, is not realizing the dignity of our pets still needs protecting. Pet hospice care is all about offering comfort, while still protecting our pets' dignity.

Our pets still have desires, and they still have needs that should be met. Little things, such as sitting with them outside, means so much to your pet. Keeping them clean, bathing them, brushing their hair, clipping their nails, and trimming their hair at home, and keeping their bedding clean and odor free, and simply offering them unconditional love and acceptance are all things your pet needs from you. These are all things that should not stop, just because your pet is nearing the end of his life. You may have to change the *way* you do these things, but you do not have to stop doing them. Your pet *needs* you to do these things. They need to feel as though they are still important enough to you to do these things. They still have the desire to be clean and groomed. They do not want to have to lie in soiled bedding, and they should not have to. They do not want the odor on them from their urine, and they should not have to live with it. It is not their fault. It is a normal part of life, and one in which all of us will go through at some point. Care for your pet with the same love and gentleness, the same quality of care you would want, if it were you.

When caring for your pet, it is also important that you keep the area clean. Keeping a clean, and positive environment will help your pet maintain a positive outlook during this time, and will help you maintain a positive outlook as well. It is important that we keep our pets as happy and positive as we possibly can during this time in order that they may approach the end of life in a positive way.

Our pets have a need to please us. It is so important, that we let them know, that we are not disappointed in them, that we understand, and we are there for them, and that we love them, no matter what. They need our constant reassurance, that nothing is too much trouble for them, and they need to know, that we do it gladly, with a pure and loving heart. Our pets understand our word more than we realize, and they understand our actions.

Pets know when they are loved. They also know when you are upset, angry, or stressed. It is important you keep all negative energy away from your pet. Like an innocent child, when you are upset, they believe it is their fault. It makes them very sad, and it breaks their heart. The most important part of their world is you. They want to please you. They feel as though they have failed, if they cannot do this.

Take time to breathe deeply. Take a walk. Read a book. Use the times they are resting to take a nap yourself, or do something just for yourself. By taking care of yourself, you will be better equipped to offer your beloved pet the very best of care, and avoid situations which create stress in your life, and that of your pet.

I will never forget the look of sadness on Timothy's face the first time he soiled his bedding. He gently barked to let me know what had happened. Upon approaching him, he hung his head in shame. He thought he had let me down. He thought he had done something wrong. He was embarrassed, and he was ashamed. As I changed his bedding, and offered a gentle sponge bath in the middle of the night, I kept reassuring him, ever so gently, that nothing was too much trouble. I praised him several times each day, and reminded him, how very much I loved him, and how very blessed I was to have him in my life. I meant every word. I could have cared for him like this forever, and I would not have minded a single bit. I told him every day, how very valuable he was in my life. I put my time and energy into simply loving him, caring for him, and nurturing him. He was worth it to me. He deserved to be love and nurtured, and he deserved to have his dignity protected to the very end. Not once was it a burden. It was an absolute privilege.

Chapter Four
Making arrangements for care

When my Dad was facing the end of his life, it did not happen at a convenient time. I was trying to work part time, and had just embarked upon the decision to return to school to earn my degree. As situations became more complex, so did the decisions I had to make.

My Dad lived out of town in the beginning stages. I was traveling on weekends in order to visit with him, returning Sunday evenings to get ready for the following week. Hurricane Katrina began a turmoil inside that was sure to threaten everything I had set out to accomplish. Many critical care patients were left alone to fend for themselves, while doctors and nurses left them uncared for, in order to flee to safety. Many of these patients lost their lives. It was the single, most horrific action I had ever heard of and it hit way too close to home.

A few short weeks following, another hurricane was scheduled to hit. A category 5, targeted to be a direct hit to the town in which my father was hospitalized. Traffic was already shut down, making it impossible for anyone to enter. I made numerous calls to the hospital, each one ending in them reassuring me, they would relocate my father.

It was Thursday. The hurricane was scheduled to hit on Friday evening, and my Dad was still at the hospital. He had not yet been relocated, and I was beginning to panic. They had assured me he would be relocated in plenty of time, though my faith was dwindling.

The following day, he was still there. I called almost non-stop. I begged. I pleaded. I cried. When all of these things failed, I resorted to threatening with lawsuits. My father was 72 years old, and was terminal. I was told FEMA had taken over evacuations, and I feared the value of his life would be determined by his age, and prognosis. I let the hospital know my fears, and reminded them they had no right to determine the value of his life. Yes, I threatened to own that hospital should anything happen to my father.

I am not proud of the way I acted. Under any other circumstances, I would have handled things more calmly. I also, was not willing to be passive regarding the care and well-being of my father. It was 2:30 pm; - A few short hours away from the hurricanes' scheduled appearance. The hurricane had not changed courses, and my father was still there. The last conversation with the nurse at the hospital, suggested I do whatever I could do on my own, to arrange for transportation for my father.

I immediately called a hospital in my city, which I knew had a helicopter, and asked for their assistance. I was ready and willing, to put everything on the line at this time. Nothing else mattered. At this point, I would have given my home, my car, and anything else I had of value, just to insure my Dads' safety.

Within a few short minutes, he was airlifted from the hospital, and shortly thereafter, landed safely at a hospital six hours away from where we lived. I immediately packed a bag, and was in my car, on my way to the hospital to see my Dad. At that moment, nothing else mattered. The only thing that mattered to me was that my Dad was safe, that he knew I was aware where he was, and what was going on in his care. School did not matter. I could pursue that any time. Work did not matter. God would provide. What did matter, was my Dad.

I do not know if my actions had anything to do with my Dad being so quickly airlifted to safety after my call for help. Possibly, it was a coincidence. Possibly, God had already made these arrangements. Whatever the reason, I do believe in faith, and I do believe, when we place so much of our time and energy into accomplishing something that is important to us, God meets that faith, and He will make it happen.

I faced a similar dilemma months later. After the hurricane had passed, my sister finally convinced the insurance company to allow him to be hospitalized closer to where we lived. I had choices to make.

I was honest and frank with my employer, and my need to spend as much time with my Dad as I possibly could during this time. I spoke with the counselor at the college, explaining my reasons to withdraw. I was pleasantly surprised at the understanding I received during this time, and the willingness of my employer to allow me to do what I needed to do for my Dad.

During the first two stages of Timothy's health decline, I did the best I could to keep up with my daily work activities, while still being able to tend to his needs. My mom, in her love and graciousness, cared for him when I had to leave to go to work. I worked as much as I could from home in order to be there with him. Not wanting to disrupt her normal routine of planned weekly outings, I scheduled the times I had to leave the house around her schedule. It was not always easy, but we made it work, and we did it very effortlessly. As his health continued to decline, I made a choice. I wanted to be home with him. I wanted to be there for him. I did not want him to wonder where his mommy was. I wanted to care for him. I wanted to be the one to nurture him. I wanted to be the one to sponge bathe him after he soiled his bedding, and I wanted to be the one to comfort him.

I had tried juggling the two, but my heart was with my beloved pet. I opted to be honest and frank with my employer, knowing I was placing myself in a position of vulnerability in my job. I hoped they would understand, but regardless, this was my position. I took a leave of absence from work in order to be home with my beloved pet. To my surprise, it was accepted, without qualm.

Worry began to surface. How would I pay my bills? How would I continue to live without a paycheck coming in? I did not have the answers. As I reasoned it out, I realized how very insignificant my worries had become. I may have to make payment arrangements with the bill collectors. If this took longer than expected, I may have to find another job. There were solutions to all of the worries I had. They may not be the ideal solutions, but they were indeed solutions. I had nothing to worry about. My worry was unfounded, and it only took away the time I needed to focus on caring for my beloved pet. Money can be replaced. This time in his life, can never be replaced.

I prayed for peace, and God granted it. I prayed for God to comfort us in our time of need, and He provided it. I prayed for provision, and He made it happen. I prayed for guidance and wisdom as I cared for my beloved pet, and it was there. I prayed for the strength and courage to write this book, and He gave it. The solutions are there, if only we dare to find them.

I would encourage anyone who truly wishes to be a part of the end of life care of their pet, to find solutions. If you have sick days or vacation time from your job, consider taking advantage of this time, especially during the last two stages of your pets' life. This is when your pet will need you the most. The final two stages tend to progress relatively quickly, often lasting only a couple of weeks.

Not everyone has jobs who offer paid time off or sick time, and taking this time of would often mean an inability to pay your bills on time if you do not have savings enough to cover your expenses. Even so, there

36

are creative ways of dealing with bill collectors during this time, should you wish to spend this time with your pet, especially in the latter stages. The key is to be proactive.

Call them ahead of time, and let them know you need an extension, or need to miss a payment. Ask credit card companies to place a payment at the end of the note. Explain to them there has been a family emergency, and you will not have the funds this month. You do not have to go into detail as to what the family emergency is.

As an alternative, ask them to break this month's payment up in installments you can afford later, once you are back at work on your regular schedule. Utility companies will normally always work with you on payment arrangements, extending the payment deadline or making payment arrangements that you can afford. Mortgage companies will usually allow you to put a payment on the end of the note at least once per year. Yes, you will pay extra interest in the long term, but it will allow you a month of not worrying about how your house payment will be made, and free up funds to last you through the month when you are not receiving a paycheck. While renting, this becomes trickier, as most property owners are not so understanding. You will be required to pay your rent, however if you can get extensions on the other bills, it will still be of great help. This will help in allowing you the time you need to care for your beloved pet without worrying about bills. It is not the ideal solution of course, but it is indeed a solution if you truly want to be available for your beloved pet. If these solutions are not possible in your situation, you can check into other potential solutions.

Explore other options. Involve other family members or friends who love your pet, and arrange for them to help in your pets' care. Call your veterinarians' office, and

ask if there is a technician who may want to ea
little extra money caring for your hospice pet w...
are away. Do an online search for pet hospice homes, or
pet hospice caregivers in the area. Is there a pet hospice
volunteer program in your community, or a pet hospice
home that could care for your pet? Some, will even offer
payment arrangements if you do not have the complete
fee in the beginning. For pet parents who just cannot take
off work during the final stages when care is most
needed, getting help while you are at work, or entering
your pet into a pet hospice home is an excellent and
loving alternative.

    If you choose to offer home hospice care for your pet,
there are a few inexpensive items you will need, most of
which you probably already have on hand, or can
purchase very inexpensively. By having these supplies
readily available, it will make things much easier as the
need presents itself. You will use these items most
frequently during the care of your hospice pet. Some are
optional, while others are crucial to the success of
offering loving and nurturing care to your pet.

Supply List

1. 2-3 blankets (for offering clean bedding at all
    times)
2. disposable bed pads w/plastic backing
3. Hair brush (for grooming)
4. Hair clipping (for grooming)
5. Nail clippers Towels
6. Dish pan (for sponge baths)
7. Wash cloths (for sponge baths and cleaning eyes)
8. 81 mg baby aspirin, the chewable kind- NOT
    enteric coated
9. Prescription pain medication from veterinarian

10. Chamomile tea bags (optional) for relaxation
11. Lavender essential oil (optional) for relaxation
12. Soft food for easy digestion
13. Shallow water bowl
14. Pet slide (see previous chapters on how to make)
15. Comfortable bed (see below on how to make)
16. Garbage bags or other plastic to cover bedding
17. Small trash can w/lid (for soiled bed pads)
18. Baby rash ointment for anal area
19. Flea collar – no flea drops or flea prescriptions (if needed)
20. Disposable gloves (optional)
21. Hand sanitizer
22. Mild aroma disinfectant for floors
23. Antiseptic body cleanser/perineal cleanser-for sponge bathing and anal and perineal cleaning.
24. Ramp (optional) for larger pets
25. Activity chart – very important
26. Letter from veterinarian – very important

Blankets

Having a minimum of two blankets, preferably three will insure you pet will always have a fresh, clean blanket to lie upon. It can be accomplished with two; however, there will be times when the other blanket is still in the dryer when needed. By having three blankets, it will help you avoid those situations where maybe the other blanket is not fully ready for use.

Disposable bed pads

Disposable bed pads with the plastic backing are readily available at most any store, including grocery stores, and are much less expensive than pet training pads. These will help tremendously during the latter stages, when your pet is no longer capable of going outside to the bathroom. They are also very helpful, in keeping the laundry down to a minimum.

During the last two stages of life, you can expect that your pets' body will be cleansing itself of excess waste and urine, usually in small amounts. They still need to be kept clean with fresh bedding supplied. Using the bed pads provide a way to keep the bedding clean and dry, only needing to change the actual bedding in the mornings, and usually once throughout the day.

Hairbrush

It is important for your pet to know they are still worth grooming. It is very healthy for their self-esteem, knowing they are loved and cared for.

Just as humans, when we are cared for and nurtured, when our hair looks neat and we are clean, we feel better naturally. It is important to keep your pet feeling good about themselves, and gentle grooming is a big part of this. Brush ever so gently, as their little bodies are more sensitive during this time.

Hair clippers

You do not have to be a professional groomer to use the hair clippers on your pet. It is very important that you keep the hair at the anal area clipped in order to prevent infection when they have bowel movements, and to make it easier to keep them clean and odor free. Once they get to the place in their journey, when their bowl movements will occur lying down, keeping the anal area clipped will help prevent the waste from becoming imbedded in their fur.

Nail clippers

Your pets' nails may need trimming at least once or twice during their journey. If you are nervous about doing this, there are a few other options. Consider filing them instead with an emery board. If they are long, you may want to invest in nail clippers, which have a laser on them, which turns green if you are in the safety area and red if you are too close to the quick. If you have other pets, or plan to get another pet, this would be a good investment that could save you grooming expenses later on.

Towels

It is a good idea to have a ready supply of 2-3 towels available for drying your pet after sponge bathing. Blow-drying is also acceptable; however, they will still need towel drying prior to blow-drying.

Shallow dishpan

Having a shallow dishpan dedicated for sponge baths is a very economical way of keeping your pet clean. Always use luke-warm water, and add a small amount of antiseptic shampoo to the water. If you do not have antiseptic shampoo, regular shampoo for pets that is gentle, is fine to use. Do not use a medicated shampoo. It is too harsh for their system during this time, and may contain camphor, which will not comforting to your pet.

Wash cloths

Your pet will need a supply of wash cloths close by for single use per incident. It is a good idea to provide a clean washcloth for each sponge bath, and a clean separate washcloth for cleaning their eyes with warm water.

Pain Medication

Having pain medication available before your pet actually needs it can make their transition much easier, and help them get much needed rest. Ask your veterinarian for a prescription of liquid pain medication for your pet early into the transition in order to have it on hand. In the beginning, often times 81mg of baby aspirin is all they need. Some pets do well with just the baby aspirin. Be sure you get the chewable kind, and not the enteric-coated baby aspirin. More than likely, when your pet truly needs the pain medication the most, he will have stopped eating, so you will not be able to mix it into their food. You will need to administer pain medication using a medicine dropper or a syringe-type oral dispenser. If using baby aspirin, you can dissolve it in a small amount of water, and place it in a dropper or syringe-type oral dispenser for administering. Always check with your veterinarian for dosage on baby aspirin. The standard dose is 5mg-15mg per pound every 12 hours. 10mg per pound I have found to be a safe place, though I normally begin with the least amount that will control the pain, and increase to the maximum safety dosage if needed. Not all pets require prescription pain medication, though having in on hand is important should you not be able to keep your pet comfortable otherwise. Comfort is very important in hospice care.

Chamomile tea

A weakened solution of chamomile tea is very useful in aiding your pet to calmness during their transition, and helps them with rest that is more comfortable. I also found, it helps in aiding with digestion during the second and third stage, and is useful for mild pain. Brew a cup of chamomile tea and allow it to cool. Add it to their water bowl, at approximately a quarter cup of tea to 1 cup of water.

Lavender Essential oil

A few small drops of lavender essential oil on your pets' blanket are very calming, and are helpful with rest that is more peaceful. A little goes a long way. One drop on each corner of the blanket is normally all you will need. Too much can cause stomach upset.

Soft high quality food

Serving your pet dry food during this time could be very difficult on your pet, and could cause them additional pain as their digestive system begins to slow

42

down. By providing high quality soft food, your pet will be more able to digest their food intake. Once your pet slows down on eating pet food, you may offer boiled chicken with some cooked rice, making sure you cut the chicken to a fine consistency.

Shallow water bowl

During the final stages of your pets' life, it will be more difficult for them to drink water on their own. At some point in the latter stages, you will need to hold their head to help them drink the water they are still craving and needing. Having a shallow water bowl will enable your pet to drink water more easily, and help prevent spills on their blanket. It will also help when they can no longer help support their head while drinking, during a time when you will be supporting their head alone.

Pet slide for transport (larger pets)

For medium to larger breeds, a pet slide will come in very handy in transporting your pet outside to the bathroom during the early stages. I would very highly recommend you spending the time and small amount of funds to provide this safe alternative of transport for your pet, if you have a ramp to slide it up and down. You can very easily, and inexpensively build a ramp, on a small scale, and it will be very much worth the investment. You can always remove it once the need is no longer present.

When offering hospice care to medium to larger breeds, having a ramp will prove to be the safe and easy alternative to transport during the first few stages.

Comfortable Bed/Garbage bags

Comfortable bedding is very important during your pets' illness and transition. Being unable to move around as much as they used to, they will be resting most of the time. Their bones and muscles will become sore, and bones are much more fragile. You do not need to buy an expensive pet bed. A foam egg-crate type mattress pad will work just fine. Cut it to the size needed, and double it. Slip it into a large garbage bag, and secure the ends to prevent it from becoming soiled. Cover with one of the blankets.

Small garbage can with lid

This will come in very handy especially during the latter stages of your pets' life, when you will be using the disposable bed pads. Place a garbage bag in the can, and use this to dispose of your soiled bed pads. Keeping the lid on prevents odor in your home, until the bag is full and taken out, and is replaced. Keeping it nearby will make things much easier on you when the time needed presents itself.

Baby rash ointment

During the latter stages, when you pet can no longer go outside to the bathroom, it is not uncommon for raw spots to appear at the rear leg/hip area where your pet has been lying down. It can very easily become raw and painful, especially when being exposed to urine or waste. It is very important then to keep our pets' bedding clean and dry and sponge bathe them after each bedding change. After a sponge bath, apply a layer of the ointment to these areas to prevent further redness and soreness, prevent infection, and provide a protective barrier.

Flea Collar

Placing flea drops or giving flea pills to a sick pet is like placing fuel on a fire. It is not recommended. You can, however if necessary, purchase a flea collar for your pet to prevent flea infestation during this time, and keep your pet more comfortable.

Disposable gloves

Disposable gloves are a good idea when cleaning urine and feces and are just good sanitation. Otherwise, be sure you wash your hands before and after each encounter with your pet with a high quality disinfectant soap.

Hand Sanitizer

It is always a good idea to have a supply of hand sanitizer on hand. Use it before and after handling your pet. The last thing in the world they need is more germs that could possibly compound the issue they are already having. It will also help prevent you from spreading germs to or from other pets in the home.

Disinfectant for floors

Keeping your floors clean and sanitized is very important to the overall health of your pet and your family. It also helps to create a more positive environment for everyone, and prevents germs from building up and spreading. An ideal solution would be a steam floor cleaner, which is even healthier for all concerned. In the absence of this, a good disinfectant, which is not too harsh smelling, is an excellent choice. Bleach is excessively harsh and is not recommended for hospice pets.

Antiseptic body cleanser/perineal cleanser

It is a good idea to purchase an antiseptic body or perineal cleanser for your pet. While sponge bathing, apply the perineal cleanser to a damp washcloth, and gently wash the perineal area, and the anal area, rinsing in between. You can also use the perineal cleaner for body washing. Most perineal cleaners are no rinse formulas, so there is no worry about leaving soap behind. You can find a gentle effective perineal cleaner at most drug stores, which are perfectly safe for your pet.

In the absence of a perineal cleaner, a good quality pet shampoo is fine. For odor and disinfecting of the pets' coat, you can mix a few drops of lemon, a few drops of orange, along with a few drops of rosemary in a fine mist water bottle, and gently spray on your pet and work through their hair. You can also use this in the water with your sponge bath solution.

Ramp

Since medium to larger breeds will prove more challenging to safely transport, a ramp will be very helpful during those first two stages, when you are taking them for regular bathroom breaks. A temporary ramp can be built very inexpensively, and will prove to be a lifesaver. It will make it easy to transport your pet on the pet slide. It does not have to be appealing. You can always remove it later once it is no longer needed. The goal is to make it functional, and give you a way to transport your larger pet safely.

Activity Chart

This is one of the most important tools you will need from the very beginning. It will enable you to track changes and behaviors in your beloved pet. It is also a very useful and necessary tool as others offer care to your pet in your absence. The veterinarian will find this chart extremely useful and helpful in prescribing medication for your pet. An activity chart will allow you to know everything that is going on with your pet, and give you clear indications as to the progression of your pets' journey.

Letter from veterinarian

It is important that in the beginning of choosing pet hospice care, that you receive a letter of approval from your veterinarian to offer home pet hospice care to your pet. Your veterinarian will require you to work with them as a team, assuring your pet has ample pain medication, and may require home visits periodically to insure your pet is being cared for properly. You will also need to keep in contact with your veterinarian on a weekly basis, advising them of the progress of your pet. Always have your activity chart completed for your veterinarian. This will insure they have correct information available and a clear picture of what your pet needs in order to remain comfortable during this time. It will also help them to offer you the advice and support you need during this time, and insure you are maintaining a positive outlook toward pet hospice care. Remember that your veterinarian is concerned with the overall well-being and humane care of your pet. It is important when embarking upon hospice care, that you have their full support, and that you are following the necessary guidelines in offering home hospice care to your pet. Home hospice care for your pet is never intended to be a substitute for proper veterinarian care, but an alternative to euthanasia. Please do not attempt to offer home hospice care for your pet without the knowledge and acceptance of a qualified veterinarian who is familiar with Pet hospice care.

Chapter Five
Other Pets in the Home

During Timothy's illness, our "roly-poly" feline remained an amazing comfort. He decided on his own, to take on the roll of caretaker, planting himself in the dining room, which is where we kept Timothy, since it was the closest to all the family activities.

Each time I approached Timothy to offer him care, comfort, or attend to one of his needs, our sweet little feline baby was right there. I noticed that in part, he was interested in being a part of what was going on. He also, needed to be reassured, that he was still loved, and still important. He could see all of the added attention being focused on Timothy. He was not jealous in any way. He was very loving and gentle during this time. I believe he understood. I also believe that he too, needed some additional comfort and attention. It was difficult for him too.

Though there were times when I was changing bedding, I had to gently pick him up and remove him from being quite so close to the area, I also realized his desire to help and be a part of the daily routine of caring for Timothy. I also realized he was feeling a little insecure. By taking the time to pick him up often, hold him, and keep him brushed and cared for as well, he was much happier, and it made him so much more comfortable and accepting of the extra time I was devoting in caring for Timothy.

He was also aware, I am convinced, that Timothy was very sick, and he too, needed the extra attention to help get him through the difficult time of seeing the health of his beloved family member decline. Our pets are very perceptive, and they too, grieve, just as we are grieving.

As Timothy's condition progressed, our beloved feline baby had planted himself near him in the dining room. We had to bring his litter box into the area as well, because he was soiling the carpet nearby. He did not want to leave the area long enough to walk to the other part of the home where his litter box was located.

Day and night, that is where he stayed, never leaving the area in which Timothy was. Many times, he would fall asleep, right next to Timothy, as if to comfort him.

After Timothy passed, he too grieved. He was confused at first, and I noticed him looking around, as though wondering where Timothy was. He continued to stay in that area of the house as though not wanting to leave.

I placed a second litter box in my bedroom, and began taking his food and water in the bedroom with me at night, gently picking him up to come to bed when I retired for the evening. He was very happy with this solution, and within a few weeks, was back to his old self, of roaming around the house as normal.

We continue to grieve together to this very day. I would encourage you to allow your other pets the freedom to be a part of things, being careful not to scold them for their curiosity and desire to be a part of things. There are indeed those times when their involvement may interfere in the care at a particular time, and yes, they need to be gently removed from the area. It is equally important that once you have completed the task, that you go to them and offer them the love, affection, and reassurance they need.

Chapter Six
The Final Stages

You will without a doubt, know the difference. Although your pet had been slowing down on his consumption of food, eating only small amounts rather than his full meal, this time is different. He is not interested. This is the beginning of Stage 3. This is a relatively short phase, often lasting no more than a week and possibly up to two. Care is very easy at this time. Before the end of this phase, you will no longer be taking them outside to use the bathroom. They will no longer be interested in food. Most of their time is spent sleeping. They will need water, occasional bedding changes, sponge baths, and lots of love. They still recognize your voice. They will still attempt to wag their tails when they hear you speak. They want your love, and they need your presence.

They will experience more labored breathing during this time. They are beginning to experience more pain, though it is very manageable with pain medication. Heavy, deep breathing, flapping their tail, and panting are all indications they need pain medication. Give it to them. Do not withhold pain-relieving medication.

Each pet is an individual with different thresh-holds for pain. At this time, some will only require a low dose to manage their pain, and still keep them alert during this time. Lavender on the corners of the blanket helps to assist in relaxation. Chamomile tea is also very useful during this time. They will continue to expel the remainder of the contents left in their colon, though they have not eaten. This will be in small amounts, often no more than a tablespoon or two at a time. Urine will have a stronger odor than normal. They will have less strength, often unable to keep their heads raised for long periods.

If you do not have a letter from your veterinarian on hand by this time, stating you are offering home hospice care for your pet now is the time to get this. Ideally, you should have this on hand from the beginning. The letter should state and describe the potential appearances onlookers may see in your pet. This is a precautionary measure, but one that is well worth it. For those who do not understand home hospice for pets, they may not understand why your pet is losing weight rapidly, and may not understand that what you are doing is in the best interest of your beloved pet. By having this statement signed by your veterinarian, it will protect you from any potential accusations.

Your pet may seem to look into the air, as though they are seeing something the rest of us cannot see. They may sometimes begin to bark, as though they are talking to someone in the distance. At times, in their slumber, you will see their little legs moving, as if they are running. They may twitch, and make little noises in their sleep. This is a normal part of the process, as they are beginning to get a glimpse of a new life that is waiting for them.

During this time, their bodies are beginning to function without food. They no longer need food as they once did. They are receiving spiritual nourishment. Their bodies are going through the spiritual journey of preparing for their final days on this earth.

When the time approaches that your pet no longer desires food, you may offer them boiled chicken, with a little rice mixed in, making sure you cut the chicken in very small pieces. This will be short lived, as before long, food will not interest your pet at all. You can also try chicken broth if they will not eat any food. Do not be alarmed. This is a natural part of the process, and your pet knows what it needs. Do not attempt to force-feed them. Offer them food frequently, and respect their wishes if they refuse.

It is very normal, that your pet will begin wasting, losing weight quickly, with bones protruding, especially in the rear hindquarter area. Grooming will be more challenging, and will be done in their bed. Having the plastic beneath the bedding and the disposable bed pads in place will assist in keeping the bedding dry while offering sponge baths.

There is a lot going on with your pet right now. They are beginning to realize, that they may not get better. They are beginning to realize, that something is seriously wrong, and beginning to accept that soon, they may be leaving you behind.

They still have the desire to please you. They still want to be able to go to the bathroom outside as they have been taught, though at this point, they cannot support themselves at all. It worries them they cannot get to the door to let you know they have to go potty.

When they have to go to the bathroom, they may bark or whimper as they are lying down. They may become restless, and begin trying to scoot off their bed. You will often find them off their blanket in another area of the room. They have crawled to get to their water bowl, or have crawled away from their bedding, in an attempt to get to the door to use the bathroom. They did not want to soil their bed. You may find them, lying in their urine or feces, as they attempted to do the right thing. They are disappointed in themselves, and they feel ashamed.

They need your compassion. They need your reassurance. They need you to tell them, that it is okay. They need to know, that you will gently lift them out of their mess, and lovingly clean their bodies, and place them on a clean, fresh, comfortable bed. They need to know you will bring them their water when they are thirsty. They need you to sit with them, speaking words of comfort and love, and gently stroke their little head until they fall asleep. They need your loving and gentle voice, telling them how very special they are, and that they are worth everything to you. They need you to tell them, that they could never disappoint you. They need to know you still love them, and how much joy they still, bring into your life, just by their presence.

Love knows no boundaries, and love is unconditional.

Some pets at this stage will still not be comfortable urinating or having bowel movements in their bed, in spite of the disposable bed pads being placed beneath them. They still have such a strong desire to please you that they will continue to crawl off their bedding. This is something new to them, and in spite of their weakened state, they still have a desire to do the right thing. You can take them outside during this time if you prefer, however you need to be aware, that they will be unable to stand at all on their own. You will need to fully support them as they urinate, and bowel movements are usually done in a lying down position. You also need to be very gentle with them, as their bones are very fragile, and could break very easily. It will not be long, they will realize the labor involved in being lifted and taken outside. It is hard on their bodies. They will soon realize on their own, they can no longer do this.

During this time, by encouraging pets to relieve themselves in bed, you can create a much safer environment. They need to come to terms with this new way, which goes against their natural instincts, and everything they were taught. They need to know you will respond quickly, to changing the soiled pads beneath them, and gently clean their bodies. It is not uncommon, for them to become restless, and begin barking and whimpering when they need to use the bathroom during this time. This can last several minutes each time, until they are finally able to relieve themselves. They are uncomfortable, both emotionally, and physically. Often, they will begin moving around, and attempting to crawl in order to exercise themselves enough to help them move their bowels. Gentle massage of the abdominal area often helps, along with sitting next to them, gently stroking their little heads, and offering words of comfort. Laying on of hands also is beneficial. Once they have their bowel movement, it is important for you to scoot them away from it, and change the bed pads beneath them. You will also want to offer a sponge bath to the anal area to remove any feces, which may have gotten into their hair.

Reassurance and unconditional love is very important during this time. They feel as though they are letting you down. It is very important you assure them that they are not letting you down, and that it is okay. They need lots of praise during this time, so give it freely and abundantly. Let them see you smile at them when you look at them. Speak only words of life and love to them.

Although your pet has stopped eating, they will have an increased thirst during this time. It is important you continue to offer fresh water to them on a regular basis. They will sleep more than usual, though are very thirsty upon awakening. They will often wake up just long enough for a drink. They need someone with them at virtually all times from this point forward.

They will begin to weaken quickly. You will have to hold their head when drinking water. You will need to turn them over, approximately every two hours if they are awake. By keeping your activity chart current, you can often determine a pattern of behavior of your pet, and the period is which you can focus on other things while they are sleeping. Keep in mind, that in the end, their needs are very sporadic, so the activity chart is not always accurate as their pattern can change at any time. As a rule, during this time, they will need someone available approximately every hour and a half, to every two hours. This is a general idea, and it can change at any time.

During this time, their bodies are doing things they have no control over, so there is no way to truly determine time frames. It is best to have someone available to your pet at all times, who will be dedicating to responding quickly to his or her needs.

Imagine being totally dependent upon someone else, and having to wait hours for someone to return to have your need met. I pray that anyone offering hospice care to a pet would be sensitive to the physical and emotional needs of their pet and even potential needs of their precious pet, during this sensitive time.

Keeping your pet turned regularly is very important to their comfort. They will normally let you know when they need to be turned during stage three. You may notice them attempting to turn themselves, struggling in the process. Though a smaller pet may be turned more easily, larger breeds will be more challenging. One way I have found that works extremely well is to have another blanket nearby, laying next to the blanket your pet is lying upon. Place the second blanket to the back of your pet, never to the front where their legs are.

From the back, gently place your hands beneath your pet, and gently scoot them to the end of their blanket, closer to the new fresh blanket. Facing their back, gently reach over, and lift the blanket they are lying on from the front, allowing your pet to gently roll onto the fresh blanket, using one hand to place beneath your pet as they roll and using the other hand to gently lift the blanket. Once your pet is on the fresh blanket, from the back again, gently place your hands beneath your pet and distribute them more evenly onto the fresh blanket. Depending upon the size of your pet and their pet bed, this can sometimes be achieved using the same blanket if you get your coordination down correctly.

Lifting your pet

Lifting a medium to large breed pet requires two people to be done comfortably and safely. With your pet on a blanket, you will be creating a "sling-type" lift, holding the corners of the blanket while lifting your pet. Always place your pet down gently. Remember they are very fragile during this time, both physically and emotionally. Gentleness is the key. If another person is not available, gently placing your hands beneath your pet and sliding him or her is your best and safest option.

Chapter Seven
Completion of the spiritual journey

As your pet approaches the completion of their spiritual journey toward their final destination, food has not interested them in quite some time. Most of their time is spent sleeping, and they are awake for shorter periods. In the early part of this stage, they still have a desire for water. Water should be at luke-warm temperature. Their bodies cannot accept water that is too cold at this time. This is the shortest phase of your pets' final journey, often lasting a week or less.

You will need to gently lift their head and hold them up in order to allow them to drink water. They will not be able to get up, or hold themselves up, and will not be able to assist you in any way. A shallow water bowl will be very beneficial at this time. Blankets may become saturated with water, as you are giving them water while in their bed. Keeping a towel nearby to place under the bowl when being offered will help prevent this. Do not leave your pet unattended drinking water. They cannot hold their heads up, and you will need to watch that their nose does not get into the water bowl.

Your pet may sleep for shorter periods, and are often restless. By being sure you are administering pain medication in a dropper on a regular basis, this will help these things to subside, and address any pain issues they may be having. Lavender drops on their blanket will also be beneficial. This will help give them the rest they need.

Continue to turn your pet frequently and realize signs of thirst. Often times, they will lick their lips when they need water, often in a half-asleep, half-awake frame of mind.

The final phase

Rather quickly into the final phase, they will refuse water. Their bodies no longer desire, nor need it. When this occurs, the end of their journey is very near, often within a few hours, to possibly a day.

Keep your pet warm, clean, and dry. Their bodies are very limp. This is part of the normal transition. Their bodies will be cooler to the touch. They cannot assist you in any way while moving or turning them.

You will be changing bed pads and bedding, by gently lifting each end of your pet in order to do so. Continue to keep them dry and comfortable. They have already expelled most of their bowels and urine during this time and there is little left to do.

Keep your pet covered with a blanket. Sit with them, talk with them, gently pet them, and tell them how much you love them, but that it is okay. Allow your pet to leave without guilt of leaving you behind, and without worry. Comfort them, and love them, to the best of your ability until they take their final breath.

I remember the conversation with my pet the day before he took a turn for the worse. It was on a Friday evening, when I began to notice Timothy was in need of pain medication. I told him how very much I loved him. I told him how very much he meant to me, and thanked him for all of the unconditional love and joy he had brought into my life for so many years. I also asked his forgiveness for those times in his life, I was unable to understand his needs, or had mistakenly failed to be the best mom I could be. I also told him, that as much as I loved him, that God loved him even more. I told him it was okay, and that I would see him again. I talked to him about a new life, where he would be free from pain, and once again be made whole. I also explained that although

I would not be there now; I would see him again soon. For the first time, I saw him cry. Tears came streaming down his little face and mine as well. I assured him, and myself, that this was not good-bye, but just "see you later". It was the most difficult and most painful conversation I have ever had in my life. I also knew it was a necessary one. He understood every word, and with his gentle little vocal gestures, I understood what he was saying to me as well. He was saying, "I love you", and he was saying, "thank you". He was also sad, that he would soon have to leave me behind. He needed to be sure I would be okay.

Everything inside of me wanted to tell him to hold on a while longer. Everything inside of me wanted to beg him not to go, and everything inside of me, wanted to go with him. I did not want to let go. I was not ready to let go. Even so, I was more ready, and more prepared, than if I had chosen euthanasia. I was not happy with losing him, but I was at peace with the fact, that I was loving him, to the very end.

Being present at the end

More than anything, I wanted to be with Timothy when he took his final breath. I was present when he was born. I had delivered him, and was the first one to hold him, and the first one to offer a kiss to his sweet little cheek. I wanted to be there for his final breath as well, and I wanted to kiss his sweet little cheek good-bye.

The day before he passed away was a challenging one. I had been up much of the night, trying to keep him comfortable, and get the dosage on his medication correct. In all the time I cared for him, we only had that one bad day. That one day, I had to give him the full dosage of his pain medication in order to keep him comfortable. By this time, he was limp, almost lifeless.

It was on a Saturday, the day after my pet and I had our in depth conversation.

By the latter part of the day, he was sleeping peacefully. The following day, I awoke to see him lying there, staring at me, as though he was memorizing everything about me. As if, he wanted to keep the image of my face in his mind. I knew it was close. I felt it with every ounce of my being.

Noticing he was uncomfortable by his labored breathing and flapping of his tail, though not making a sound, I gave him pain medication. I had offered him a drink, and he had refused. I continued to offer him water, and at times, he would take one or two laps, only to pull away as I was gently holding him.

He slept for five hours straight. I kept checking on him, and his breathing, as I lay beside him, kissing his sweet little cheeks, and gently stroking his head. I wanted to linger with him forever. I could not stop kissing him, and I could not stop stroking his precious little head. I never wanted it to end. I wanted to lay there with him, snuggled close to him forever.

I finally allowed him to rest undisturbed, and lay beside him, snuggled up to his frail, limp little body, and drifted to a near slumber, afraid to drift off too deeply, in case he needed me.

A few hours later, he awoke, and I turned him over. To my amazement, he was almost able to support himself with one arm, and had raised his head some. He looked so happy, and so peaceful. We talked, and I noticed that playful look on his face as though there were something he was looking forward to. This was the first time in almost a month I had seen him look so happy. I was overjoyed, and even thought for a short while, that just maybe, I would have him with me a little longer.

As Timothy was deep in thought, I quickly went into the other room for something. I do not even remember what. I was out of the room for only a minute or two, when something pulled me back into the room with him. His eyes were glazed, as if staring into space. I spoke to him, asking him if he were okay. He did not respond. I quickly went to him, and notice his breathing was slowing down. I gently turned him into a lying down position, and spoke to him softly, gently stroking his hair. He looked at me, and let out a gentle "ruff", as though saying, "See you soon", as he took his final breath. He passed away peacefully, with his eyes still open, gazing into the afterlife.

Chapter Eight
After life has ended

I spent the next several minutes in silence, basking in the presence of God who had taken my sweet little baby home. I felt a presence, telling me to let go, to not touch him. Gods' hand was upon him at that time. I was an intrusion to this special time between him and God.

I remained in the room, though backed away for a short time until I sensed it was okay for me to approach my baby. For the last time, I lay next to my beloved pet, snuggled next to him, gently stroking his hair, and offered kisses to his cheek. This was for me. He was already gone, and had no recollection of this. I needed this, for me.

Shortly after, I made sure his bedding was clean and fresh, and I brushed his hair one final time. Covering him with a blanket, I sat with him for the next two hours before taking him for burial to his final resting place.

Removal of your pets' body

Depending upon your beliefs, desires, and resources, there are a number of ways in dealing with the removal of your pet once they have passed on. Hopefully, these arrangements were made well in advance in preparation for this time.

Choosing burial or cremation is a personal choice. Larger cities prohibit burial of your pet on your lot in town. If you have family or friends outside of the city limits, they may allow you to bury your pet on their land. There are some good pet cemeteries in most cities, though they become filled rather quickly, and space is not always available.

Cremation is another available option. Do an internet search for pet crematories. Many funeral homes will offer to come remove your pet, and offer crematory services with your pets' remains returned in an urn. Some offer communal crematory services, should you not want to keep the remains. You will also have the option of dropping your pet off to the funeral home. You will need to pay for the services rendered, however the cost is minimal. In my city, private cremation is approximately $200 with urn included. Pick-up is an extra fee, and will cost more on weekends outside of normal business hours.

If cost is an issue, and you do not wish to keep the remains of your pet, you can call ASPCA, or the local animal shelter. They will dispose of your pet in accordance to their standard practice. Your veterinarian may be able to help you with arrangements for burial, cremation, or the removal of your pet.

Should you need time to decide or make proper arrangements, you will need to keep your pet as cold as possible. They either will need refrigeration, or be laid on ice. Some pet owners, depending upon the size of their pet, have placed them in coolers on ice, with plastic between the pet and their blanket to prevent them from getting wet. Others have built an inexpensive wooden tray beneath their pet they could line with plastic and fill with ice when needing to keep their pet a day or two while making arrangements, or coming up with funds needed for burial or cremation.

It is so much easier, when these decisions have been made in advance, and possible circumstances have been planned for. It allows you to quickly make the needed calls, and put into operation, the plans that have already been made, at a time when you are not grieving.

Accepting the loss

Accepting the loss of a beloved pet, friend, and companion is never an easy process. It is indeed, a process. Grieve though you must, you must also, move forward. Accept the fact that you gave your beloved pet the care, love, and nurturing they needed to the very best of your ability, and there was nothing more you could have done with the place you were in at the time. Resist negative feelings that your best was not good enough. It was your best at the time. Though most of us have afterthoughts of what we could have done better or differently, realize that your best is your best, not someone else's best. You gave everything you had to give. Accept this, and move on. Our pets have already accepted this and they have long already forgiven any of our shortcomings.

Allow yourself to grieve

One of the most difficult things so many pet parents face in the ability to allow themselves to grieve the loss of their pets. Offering pet hospice to their pet has shown to allow the pet owner to truly enter into the grieving process, recovering sooner, with the ability to be at peace, leaving no unresolved pain behind.

By offering pet hospice care to your pet, you are assured you have done everything possible, and given your pet the opportunity to travel the spiritual journey otherwise would not have been possible. Pet hospice care provides closure that euthanasia cannot provide. Not only is it the loving thing to do for our pets, but it also allows the pet parent to be free of the guilt associated with premature euthanasia, and allows them to prepare naturally over a longer period, in preparation for the parting of their pet. It also allows their pet to come to terms with his near departure in their time, allowing them the freedom to experience the spiritual journey, which takes place at the end of life.

The first few days will be the most difficult. You may still hear the voice of your beloved pet. You may continue to go to their side, only to find they are not there, having to remind yourself, they are gone.

It is common to wake up in the middle of the night to tend to your pet, only to suddenly remember, you are not doing that anymore. There is no longer a need. This is a normal reaction during the first few days, and possibly, a week or two.

Support groups are available. I would encourage you to contact one of the many resources available on our website, should you find yourself in need of grief counseling.

Take the time you need to grieve. Take time to remember your pet, and realize that feelings will arise sporadically in normal everyday conversation, which may cause you to break out in tears out of remembrance of your beloved pet. This is a normal part of the grieving process, and soon becomes more infrequent as time passes. You have just lost a beloved member of your family, and you cannot expect to bounce back quickly. You can expect to have good days, bad days, and mixed days through the grieving process. Soon you will have more good days in a row, until eventually; your beloved pet and member of your family will be remembered with joy, sadness having been replaced by loving memories, by allowing yourself the freedom to grieve.

Other pets in the home are grieving too

It is important to realize, that other pets in the home are grieving too. They too, are going through the transition of getting use to the loss of a beloved family member. By giving them lots of love and affection during this time, you can help them to accept, and deal with the feelings of confusion and sadness over the loss of their family member. The loss they feel is very real and they too need to be comforted during this time. What you will find, is in offering your comfort to your other pets, you too, will be comforted.

Though the journey in offering home hospice care for your beloved pet that is facing the end of life on this earth can be emotionally challenging, it is important that we remember, that death, is a natural part of life. By loving your pet to the end, you have the opportunity to allow them to enter into the spiritual transition with unconditional love, and unconditional acceptance. It is one last labor of love, and the most rewarding labor of love you could ever begin to imagine.

If you are interested in training to become a pet hospice caregiver, or you would like more information regarding offering pet hospice as part of your veterinarian services, please visit our website for more information.

If you need help, support, or grief counseling for the loss of your pet, please visit our website for resources that are readily available to you. Our website also offers resources for trained home hospice pet caregivers whom I have personally worked with, and is growing all the time.

www.Pethospicecareathome.com

Made in the USA
Lexington, KY
20 July 2013